The Bee's Knees: Bipolar Poetry

C.C. Brighton

authorHOUSE®

AuthorHouse™
1663 Liberty Drive
Bloomington, IN 47403
www.authorhouse.com
Phone: 1-800-839-8640

First published by AuthorHouse   12/21/2009

ISBN: 978-1-4490-5522-6 (e)
ISBN: 978-1-4490-5523-3 (sc)

Library of Congress Control Number: 2009912678

Printed in the United States of America
Bloomington, Indiana

This book is printed on acid-free paper.

To every life
That has touched mine
And kept me going…
I love you over the moon
You know who you are…
Thank you with
the most grateful
heart.
To my dearest family
And your undying love…
Unending thanks to each of you;
I love you so much.
To my doctor
And his expertise…
Thanks for getting it right.
Thank you Jesus
For the uncommon love
We share.
You have poured through
Each life represented
Here to work a miracle in me.
To God be the
Glory.

Psalm 40:1-3
(also a song by the band U2)

I waited patiently for the Lord;
   He turned to me and heard my cry.

He lifted me out of the slimy pit,
   out of the mud and mire;
He set my feet on a rock
   and gave me a firm place to stand.

He put a new song in my mouth,
   A hymn of praise to our God.
Many will see and fear
   and put their trust in the Lord.

C.C BRIGHTON was born in a southern city. She was educated primarily at one state university in the south. She became a Christian when she was twenty. She did extensive missionary work on foreign and domestic soil in her twenties. She was diagnosed with the bipolar illness ten years ago when she was twenty-five. She went back to school to get her Master of Business Administration degree at a local university when she was thirty-three while working full time.

It is her soul passion to reach bipolar individuals through the written word of poetry to help set them free. It is her greatest pleasure to hopefully inspire those who are in the howling season to hang on and live the life that God can give them. It is an abundant life that is rich in fulfillment. It is something that she never believed she would ever experience this side of Heaven. She warmly invites you into the pages ahead where she prays that you will find peace from the burning in your mind and find life where so much death has been.

PART ONE

Beloved

Feel like a lump laying listless and slack;
A physician's cure has me calm but I feel like a lifeless quack.

I am languid and beached like a whale or a seal;
Lackadaisical and drooping can I barter or steal....

Someone else's life I crave as I bargain and I think;
These thoughts of trading places will only make me sink.

The ache runs so deep;
The tears soak my feet.

Want to soar and be a success like the rest;
So unmotivated as I try and give my best.

Fragile, as dreams unravel and depression tries to settle in;
Desperate for a normal life; O God when will it end?

I crawl to Your word and open the book;
I read the pages and I climb down from the hook.

No longer will I feel like a failure or even a castaway;
Your hand is upon me each and every passing day.

You have called me by name and have a great purpose in store.
I need not fear or worry; I know You will open each door.

Your beloved, Your beloved is one name You have for me.
Great worth I have in You and the richest fare I will see.
You promised in those pages and You showed me on that tree.

Sunbeams

Laying on a cloud;
Mind once racing is now clear.

Gazing at the Son;
O what fun!

To be in His presence;
Just being me without any pretense.

Sunbeams and oceans views;
Heart is quiet while taking in the hues.

Grandeur on every side;
The sadness has died.

Joy brims over onto creation;
I am under renovation.

The Master is molding this clay;
In the Father's hands I will stay.

Cloud nine is where I will retreat;
It is where I go to get off the street.

I will be warmed up in the fire of your Son;
My mind won't feel so torched, I won't come undone.

Seek

Bipolar thoughts are thoughts of you and you alone.
It is enough to make you cry; it definitely makes you moan.

The thoughts are always self deprecating or far too grand;
Praying for others helps but you really must take a stand.

Against this evil voice that screams day and night;
Accusing you towards yourself, keeping you from the light.

Weeping in the dark, uttering cries above;
Please make it stop so I can feel the shove...

Of You removing this thing,
From my burning brain.

I want the mind of Christ and the word says that is what
    I've got;
Most do not understand and I pray this is never their lot.

The Lord is bigger than this and His face I will seek;
I will speak life and His word when I hear those shrieks.

I will overcome the power of darkness because it was already done;
I am precious to the Almighty and to His beloved Son.

Trust in Him and He will take you on a journey or a special trip;
Far better than anything this world has to drink or sip.

So let Him open your ears to the Master's music so that it
    can replace;
Those old tapes of self and sadness, let's not make haste.

Your heart will be free and you will feel so light
Give up self obsession and walk as one with sight.

Yellow

Tropical flowers by water's edge;
Makes me feel spiritual,
I come back from the ledge.

I walk slowly through the greenery;
O the lovely scenery!

I feel drunk in a euphoric state;
Peace warms me up,
The Holy Spirit opens the gate.

Water flows over the hill;
My heart sings in rapture and I feel a thrill,
I let down my shoulders and let go of the chill.

I feel so close to God in the wild luscious earth;
I gaze up above and forget all the hurt,
I take a few turns in my yellow, flowing skirt!

The sounds of the waterfall dance in my soul;
I feel safe in the shelter and His love fills the holes.

Not afraid of the racing thoughts in the splendor of His creation;
My meds are working great and I know His hand of protection.

It is okay to be me; it is good to be me.
I will embrace it all and live totally free;
Free to be God's creature, so beautiful to see.

Peaceful

The obsessive racing thoughts that try and attack;
Must change my thinking or else I get smacked.

Been thinking this way my entire life through,
Feel like I am going mad; O God what do I do?

Each time I think something bad or untrue;
I pray for someone else or think of God's beauty.

I practice focusing on the good and what makes me smile;
It takes a lot of effort but God gets me over these trials.

New patterns will form in my mind as I stay the course;
As I get bombarded by troubled thoughts, there is always
    a choice.

I will choose to fight with God's help all the way;
A healthy mind I will have and only peaceful thoughts
    will stay.

Free from the disease of a corrupt mind;
I will keep taking each thought captive and sail joyfully
    through time!

Smashing

The luster of it all;
The wonder of the fall.

The leaves changing color;
This season is like no other.

Moods also change;
A melting mind to rearrange.

Adrenaline coursing through the veins;
Won't someone break these chains?

The crisp air and cooler months;
A beautiful life I will hunt.

The leaves fall on my face
I look up and see You through the haze.

Smashing and dazzling is Your report;
This time of mania will be rather short.

Just take my meds as I always do;
Seek His love and then I will coo.

There is no secret to what this all means;
My life has been touched and this I glean.

Two simple remedies for a burning mental state;
With the right medicine and the Master, it is never too late.

You will bloom and bud as spring appears;
Frenzy and chaos you won't have to fear.

Enjoy each season and winter too;
God has His eye on you and He will see you through.

Golden

In the darkest cavern of the abyss,
When the doctors say that they must admit;

You into the hospital to that floor,
Where many have tried to soar.

You feel cold and small,
As you walk down the hall.

You say goodbye to family and the door closes shut;
Now it is just you and you feel sick in your gut.

But please do not forget who stands beside you;
He has a plan; something more for you to do.

It will not end here; no my sweet dear
You need not worry, you need not fear.

All of this will be used for something beautiful one day;
It will be your heart's desire, I must say.

Try not to see with the physical eye,
Look heavenward, way up in the sky.

You will come through this fire as golden as the Son
Your life will be a crown of jewels when it is all said and done!

Bloom

Tiny, little, shadowy figures rest in the desert;
Dressed in dirty clothes ...even a torn skirt.

Depression tries to blanket these people;
He longs to direct them to the steeple.

Their bodies are mangled by grief and self condemnation;
They long for a cup of cold water, will they ever feel elation?

Strung out by thoughts of the past;
Must this dreadful feeling last?

Hope wants to bring health to these arid places and musty faces;
So God moves quickly, He comes and chases.

These precious ones touched by illness;
Their minds on fire, desiring stillness.

God comes quick to assuage their pain;
He alone can keep them from going insane.

He washes their cuts and dresses them up;
He combs their hair and asks them to sup.

He takes the glass from their feet;
He gives them more to eat.

They are looking so well and feeling so new;
God is calming their hearts, there is nothing He can't do.

Their misery once like a waste place is now in bloom;
Beautiful flowers in plenty, they could fill a room.

God is happy to bring these hurting ones close;
He loves His aching ones so much, right down to His toes.

He came to restore and bring gifts of healing;
We can unwrap them and dance on the ceiling!

Promise

Like a fever that festers all through this mind;
Try so hard to focus on the good, this is what I find.

Self deprecating thoughts and feelings of back breaking sorrow;
Look above to carry me through until tomorrow.

Feel like a prisoner at times to the howling in my mind;
Just want peace and quiet but must I always have to climb?

Climb and climb and hang on and hang on;
To my loving Father's hand I hold so I will never be lost or gone.

I see a rainbow and the promise that it holds;
One day will be better yet, it has been foretold.

I can say thank you now for all that was and all that is on the way;
Other lives I want to touch and pull out of the grave.

Chrysalis

I ache for God on the back side of the desert.
The torment is so strong; it feels like a blizzard.

So tired of this brain a blaze;
Want to escape from these black days.

Wonder if it will ever end;
I will trust God and not go around the bend.

I feel so raw;
I am grasping at straws.

The Lord cannot fail;
His touch will prevail.

My mind will not spin off its axis;
My name is written in His book on His list.

Up and down I go;
Back and forth to and fro.

Well-wishers think they have all the answers;
Guard your heart for this I am sure.

Only a few that are touched from His Spirit;
Will look upon your burning mind without any judgement.

Love yourself as God says to do;
Embrace every part of you.

Hug yourself when you feel blue;
Rise from the ashes, this you must do.

There is beauty forming inside that chrysalis;
Spread your wings and fly far above that abyss.

Laughter

The desert is such a dry and arid place;
I lived there for so long, such a dreadful space.

Howling for my God, the screams were so loud;
In a position like that, I would never cower.

One thing good came from my state of exile;
He made me more like Him because that is His style.

Better am I now from that trip to the sand;
I am more prepared to walk through this land.

Into His image the suffering shaped me.
It has a way of doing that; it is so good for me I see.

Only in seasons is this aloud;
Now I am full of laughter and I sing aloud.

HOORAY!

Finally at peace with where I am right now in this place;
Finally content with who I am in the race.

I can be still and enjoy each moment at a time;
No thoughts of the past or even the future for that is a crime.

Feel so free to glide through each day;
Trusting in God, what a big HOORAY!

I do not have to give my resume to everyone I meet;
I am His and I have confidence in that, what a feat.

I do not have to keep up with the status quo;
I am not of this world it says in the Bible and God makes
   me grow.

No fear of man;
I am forgiven and dance in His hands.

I walk with my head held high;
God took my shame so I can jump on clouds in the sky.

I am right where I am supposed to be;
It is amazing that I do not have to strive anymore, this I
   now see.

I am through with trying so hard;
I will let God flow through me and hand me life's cards.

I feel so much joy and so much peace in my heart;
Words cannot describe it but this is a start.

I live not according to this world's ways;
My Creator has a better plan and much happier days.

Igloo

In an igloo cold and wet;
Trying so hard not to fret.

Surrounded by chilling weather;
Would like to be a feather.

I would drift away to another day;
Always worried about where I will stay.

Where I will work;
I do not want to merely lurk.

My heart longs for life in the fullest form;
Searching for the harbor in the storm.

Love to see the famous, yellow smiley face;
Gives me hope and reminds me that God is never in a daze.

He is focused on all of my needs;
Giving me shelter, doing good deeds.

With His assistance;
I run the distance.

Far from the raging voices and screams;
Your voice is radiant, it makes me dream.

I dream and I dream;
Hopeful and trusting it seems.

God will always make a way;
He will reveal it each day.

Wonderment

The depth of what we can feel;
Like no others on earth, it almost seems surreal.

A song will stop me in my tracks;
A whirlwind of emotion, my body it will smack.

I am blown away by these mysterious feelings so deep;
It is a wonderment and into my bones it always creeps.

It takes my breath away, these songs they make my day;
No words to utter afterwards, I have nothing to say.

The music and the melodies take me to another world;
Where all I can do is weep, all I can do is twirl.

I sit and think so intensely of what matters most;
Poverty and love, the fall and the curse.

God has touched me and made me special indeed;
We will weather each storm and I will plant seeds.

All I ask is for others to live and not die;
To have a real hope, to live inside.

The madness can be beaten into submission;
Jesus can hold it at bay and your body and mind He will
  enrichen.

Bud

Here's to You and Your loving embrace;
You took it all, even the disgrace.

There need not be a stigma or anything at all;
We can fit right in with Him so you need not crawl.

His word is the key to much that is grand;
It will always help you to take a stand.

Against mental illness and all of its inferno blazing;
You will start to hunt after God, it will be a craving.

He longs to make you better;
He wrote it in each of His letters.

Let Him have His way with you;
Watch and see what He can do.

Just when you think that you are a wreck;
He shows up on your scene, right on your deck.

Put your life in His hands and bloom like a bud;
You will rise from the grave and He will wash off the mud.

Dorothy's Pocket

Laying on a lily pad;
I remember times we once had.

When I could barely crawl;
Tears fell and I would fall.

You never left my lonesome side;
All I wanted to do was hide.

I wanted to die;
I had an alibi.

You said, "No"
You had something to show.

I felt so low and so bruised;
I felt so bloody and confused.

Like a little, tiny person in a pocket;
Sheltered from the storms and the traffic.

You raised me from the ashes;
You survived the lashes.

You gave me strength;
You had people pray at length.

You sent Your Son;
When I was undone.

I can see sunshine now;
I do not know how.

You did it! You did it!
You gave me back my spirit.

Help me choose You and never forget;
I am so glad that we met.

You alone can fill this deep cavernous space in my being;
When I keep my eyes on You, then I am really seeing.

A love so strong that fire cannot change it;
A fierce grip that nothing could split.

Unique

Jesus is the one;
The one and only Son.

That took it all;
That was His call.

He is the answer to a living hell;
I search the scriptures, I search on my Dell.

His word brings the hope;
That a withering heart needs to cope.

Please turn to Him and get some relief;
Do not wait a second, for it is so sweet.

My life has such meaning, such purpose in store;
I am no longer a zombie screaming, "I can't take it anymore!"

I have excitement about what the future holds;
It will be unique, not taken from a mold.

God will see to it that all is fulfilled;
He is so faithful, He longs to do this for it is part of His will.

Cover

Running up and down the walls;
Crashing in the falls.

Rubber room of old;
Straight jackets in the cold.

Bobbed wire in the head;
Pills laying all over the bed.

Awful thoughts to extinguish;
The scriptures are what I use to distinguish...

Those thoughts of You and thoughts from below;
They were so twisted for so long I did not know.

You know all and You hold the key;
To a mind that stops raging and a mind that is free.

He can help train the mind to be fixed on what is good
    and true;
He can keep those thoughts of suicide FAR from you.

TRUST IN HIM not in what this world has to offer;
Take your meds DAILY and do not listen to scoffers.

Do not EVER self medicate;
Or harm yourself, it is NEVER too late.

Be good to you and do not fall prey;
To the enemy's schemes, he will try and trip you any given day.

Get on God's side and stay by His side;
He will guide you through the darkness and you will not die.

He defeated the devil by spilling His blood;
His warring angels will fight for you and He will cover you
   in love.

Stars

Speak words of life;
He wants a heart that is contrite.

Praise Him when you are blue;
It will lift you out of the glue.

Fix your eyes on Him;
Things won't seem so dim.

Invite Him into your broken heart;
He will remove every dart.

Don't focus on the scars;
But look up at the stars.

Far and beyond, up in the sky;
He will make it better, you will not die.

When it seems black as night;
Hold out for the light.

It will come in the morning;
His love will be warming.

Your heart it will ease;
It will be a breeze.

He can do anything;
He can make you sing!

Climb

Mental quicksand,
Can I get a better hand?

I am not ready,
For mind spaghetti.

Blinding lights that pain my eyes;
Must I lay in a room and shut the blinds?

That is when I curl up in His hand;
Father God envelopes me and helps me take a stand.

Against all the devils and the demons too;
That try to possess me or make my mind glue.

They will never win, they were defeated at the cross;
I still have symptoms of the illness but it was not a loss.

It takes an extraordinary faith to walk out each day;
Through blistering highs and lows hotter than the month of May.

I know He is proud that I am still here;
Only listen to the voices in church that clap and cheer.

Turn away from those that judge or condemn;
Protect yourself and if you have to …climb out on a limb.

God will provide comforters that will love you on the way;
Towards health and healing and the finer days.

Swirling

Jumping over puddles on the bridge;
Trying to avoid the fringe.

Peering over the ledge;
Cannot go over the edge!

It calls out to me in the night;
I must put up a mighty fight.

Must preserve this life I have;
I will jump over puddles but I must not grab..

Onto that ledge or even look down;
I want to stop wearing this frown.

I am torn by two ways to go;
I fall to my knees and cry out, "So!"

So what do I do, I feel a tug;
I just need a big Father hug.

Please put Your healing hands on my swirling mind;
Bring peace I pray, that I need to find.

I crawl up in a ball right on the street;
I see You approaching, I see Your feet.

Could You chop off my brain and replace it anew;
Toss it aside, beat it with a shoe.

"No!" You exclaim "I have divine purpose in this setup."
"Many will hear my name and be delivered by my
  cup...

The cup I drank for the world to heal;
You are a vessel that can touch and feel...

Through Your brokenness;
Others will confess..

They need more than medicine to live on the heights."
With You there is a way to live beyond the freight.

You allowed this illness to be a part of me;
Please make it redemptive and draw many to Yourself,
  that I would love to see.

Hug

The earth and His creation is something to see.
It makes me feel euphoric; it makes me hug a tree.

I get so excited but it is under wraps;
The doctor has me balanced so I will not collapse.

These deep, deep senses;
I look at the world through different lenses.

It is a lot to feel in a mad world;
I look to my Lord because I am His girl.

He knows me so well, better than all;
I turn to Him each moment, He saved me from hell.

I push through the darkness holding His hand;
I will not give in to the depression but I will look to the Man.

If I do get down which can happen to anyone
I speak promises from the word and focus on the Son.

The Man upstairs provides all that I need;
Weapons for my warfare, I could face a stampede.

Prayer and praise get me straight;
On thin ice I will not have to skate.

Toadstools

Jumping on beautiful toadstools and sliding down
  rainbows in the air;
The upside of bipolar is the mania that makes people stare.

But it is the most joy and unbelievable high;
I laugh and I laugh until I nearly cry.

I giggle and I wink while I am witty with all;
The life of the party or the social ball.

A line for everyone and cheer to go around;
Over confident and fully affirmed never down.

Swirling and twirling and leaping inside;
A lot to contain but I do not want to hide.

I want to be out for all of the world to see;
Want to connect and be so free.

But the time winds down and the feeling starts to fade;
I want to go to sleep now but I always think it is strange.

I am revving and I am revving, no sleep to be had;
The adrenaline is pumping so I am awake and very sad.

I feel insane as the hours pass by;
My mind is under siege as I take a deep sigh.

I fight and I fight to keep this darkness at bay;
Jesus is next to me and He knows just what to say.

I will come through this untouched and stronger still;
Then I will be able to help others find the shore.

Cool

Looking through a glass window;
There is a slow motion picture in my head like a show.

I will get out again once they say it is time;
Hard to be locked up in the hospital but it helps my mind.

Feel things so deep,
Music touches the soul;
It makes me want to weep,
Or to dance and leap.

Intense and obsessed,
Try to play it cool;
But it puts me to the test.

Flames burn and turn inside my mind and being;
The Lord's loving hand is all that is freeing.

It frees me from the snare and tares of darkness;
When I get out of this place, I will feel gladness.

Now it is time to go back home indeed;
My time is over and God is my lead.

He gives me such hope,
I do far better than just cope;
Rarely do I mope,
He cleans off the depression with soap.

He lifts my head and winks;
I know I will never sink.

He reminds me to always take my meds;
He tucks me in bed never forgetting to bring peace to
my head.

Zest

So much zest for life;
A song comes on you and you feel so high.

You smile and you grin;
You have come so far, you will win.

The race set before you;
That God has called you to.

Fun with the Father, it is so wild;
I twirl on His toes because I am His child.

The scary thoughts are far removed;
The summer is here and the days are now smooth.

The sun stays out longer and this is good for the mind;
I can run and play and go out to dine.

I am so thankful to be where I am;
I was pulled from the pit of fire and rescued by the Lamb.

I see others so tortured with chemical imbalance;
Longing to tell them what the Lord and meds can do to
    help make them dance.

God took all of the diseases and every illness upon Himself
    and that was the case;
But sometimes illness lingers beyond prayers and it takes
    sustaining grace.

It takes so much to walk through the oven and not take
 your life;
It is a heat and pressure so great but NEVER give up the fight.

JESUS is our comfort and He is our strength;
We are victorious in Him and we will NEVER shrink.

From all the woes and perilous fears that try and attack us
 in our mental state;
We can seek the Lord and break through the night as it is
 NEVER too late...

Prance

You will be filled with such joy;
You will be so healthy, you will want to drink soy.

God will get you that way;
He will make you smile, He will make it all okay.

He can restore a torn life;
He can make you prance on the heights.

He alone can give you a beautiful forecast;
You will want to have a party or even a bash.

So praise Him when it is dim;
Praise Him when you do not feel comfortable in your
   own skin.

Praise Him when it feels like the end;
Praise Him when you want to grin.

Praise Him whenever you can!

Rainbow

I long for a holiday;
In the month of May.

A respite of sorts;
Where I can eat lots of torts.

I can hang out with Father;
It is the richest time even more than myrrh.

We laugh and we chat and I listen to His heart;
It is during this communion that I do not feel the darts.

The fiery darts that try and pierce my mind;
They send chills up and down my spine.

But when I am with You, it all falls away;
All the voices are disarmed, there is nothing more to say.

When I dwell on You and rest in Your presence so sweet;
I actually feel peace and my heart skips a beat.

There is no enemy on earth or below that could defeat this
state of mind;
My God is my strength and He gave us the rainbow for a sign.

Of what was promised to His children;
Salvation and healing from all our worldly sins.

He is goodness and He is kindness, a victory for His people;
I love to worship Him in a group so I just look for the steeple.

Whether it is Sunday or not, He is there just the same;
Waiting to take a vacation with you to the ocean or a stream.

A good time to take your eyes off yourself by the water;
This will exonerate you from the slums and even the gutter.

Sweetest

Bursting with joy from the tips of my toes;
Feel the Holy Spirit shivers amongst all my foes.

Now I am in the sanctuary worshipping with all I have;
I kiss heaven and God tends to my wounds with a healing salve.

I love feeling this fire in my soul;
Hunting after Him and coming in from the cold.

It is just like the sweetest song
A loving embrace in the middle of a throng.

Of people who know what it means to suffer;
A hug from above will only leave you tougher.

That suffering will produce passion that burns in the night;
It will break through the howling darkness like a piercing light.

That anguish will not be wasted but it will give you closeness
with Him;
Nothing will shake that intimacy, nothing will make you dim.

Jiggy

I feel the brilliance of this madness;
It is sheer agony none the less.

I will look at the bright side; heretofore,
This condition brings me closer to God, I seek Him more
  and more.

A life dependent on God is a special one;
With purpose and strength and then some.

I am zippy and jiggy with my unique personality;
I would never trade my life, it's my own reality.

God we have walked through the blazing trail of this
  illness hand in hand;
I would never make it without You, You walk me through
  the land.

Up high on your shoulder I sit for all the world to see;
You are so very proud of me.

With Your help I am still here;
Other people I hope to inspire and steer…

Along a better path filled with grace;
Always embrace God's face.

Snatch

Never give up when you want to go down;
Down underground until there is no sound.

You must look up and see beyond the clouds;
Push onward even through the crowds.

God is right there to help you get right;
He will carry you through the darkest night.

When you cannot go any further, He will do the rest;
He wants to give you gifts from His treasure chest.

His gifts of mercy, love, and peace are to be gained;
We need only ask for them to be obtained.

We need them for the blistering journey that has been;
We must come out of the lair, come out of the den.

We must join the race and get active in the game;
He will lift us up when we are lame.

Lord You are so good; You can truly touch the unwell.
You bring them back; You snatch them from hell.

I love You for You and not Your healing touch;
Just hold me forever, I love You so much.

Princess

How could a godly woman have rage;
She acts like she has just been set loose from a cage.

It roars inside and comes crashing out;
Sometimes in the form of violence and sometimes in a shout.

The illness makes her cry over all that she does,
God attempts to calm her; He makes over her with such a fuss.

She rejects His love because she beats herself up;
She does not yet understand the dove.

The dove is the spirit of mercy and grace;
That lands on her bruised shoulder and tries to embrace.

That little wounded one who has fought and fought so hard;
To hold it together while feeling so marred.

Father comes with His love and a kiss for the head;
Her heart is so hard, it feels so dead.

She has been striving for His love for so long;
He wants her to know that He loves her and has prepared a song.

The song is in the word and it displays a marriage feast;
It is a song for a princess or even for the least.

She must hate her sin and not herself indeed;
She must forgive like He forgives her and then let Him lead.

He will take her by the hand and help her see very soon;
Even though she falters, He loves her over the moon....

Made

Razors and blades,
What I hate;
Almost my fate,
But God wasn't late.

Jesus came quick,
My wounds He would lick;
I was so sick,
He makes me live, He makes me tick.

Sharp things still haunt this mind so frail;
It hits my head hard like hail.
It makes me feel paralyzed and move like a snail;
But You died to heal me, you took all the nails.

Not in vain did you die and rise I say;
Now I live in more merry days.
I run and I play; I rest in the shade.
With You on my side, I always have it made!

Soar

Lift up His name;
When you feel insane.

Keep praising until you feel His presence on you;
This may take some time but what else can you do.

When your heart is mangled and torn into shreds;
This will bring you back from the dead.

Look at Him and do not get swallowed whole;
By all of your symptoms, come back from the cold.

The misery will come right off like a soiled garment;
You will not have to run or feel so spent.

You can feel relief and feel so free;
Praising Him will help you to see.

That even though there is an illness to bear;
There is so much life to live, you need not despair.

Take your medicine and rest your weary eyes on Him;
Your life won't be so dark or even so dim.

You need both of these remedies to leap and soar above
    the malady;
You will come to embrace and even love your new reality.

Honey

No more rock, paper, scissors on how the day will go;
I no longer have such a tough road to hoe.

God has brought me so far;
I was like a falling star.

He trusted me with suffering as I was locked up several times;
A rough place where everyone had mental land mines.

But now I am happy as a lark,
Singing after dark.

Swinging in a swing;
So glad to be friends with the King.

Jesus is the one and only;
He makes everything sweet like honey.

Hosea Love

Hosea love, Hosea love is what You have had for me;
You have loved me in my chains and helped to set me free.

Your love is amazing; it melts the rough places away.
Your love is so tender; it calms my heart on difficult days.

You are uncommon; You are love itself.
You loved me back from the edge; I was on a shelf.

I cannot believe how good You are and You stand the test
of time;
Want to be like You, want to sparkle, want to shine.

You are so worthy of my highest praise and thanks;
You rescued my bruised body from the ocean banks.

It is a love story that begins with You alone;
You found me and drew me close , now my heart is not a stone.

You are the best and You are all that I need;
I am so grateful and I hope You always take the lead.

My heart is so full of laughter and joy; it sings of merriment.
You have taken away the darkness and on a new journey
I have been sent.

Glow

Wanting to chop off this head;
Just like the dead.

Then I would not feel nails in my mind;
Or hear loud sounds like churning combines.

I will never let it have me;
No I will face it and not flee.

I need my God, my family, and my friends;
It takes them all, or else I would end.

But I will glow in the darkest night;
I will dance when the lights are out of sight.

I will triumph over this madness;
I will stomp on this sadness.

I will reach the summit;
I will tell the illness to shove it!

I thank God for my doctor and all that he has done;
He helps keep my mind clear so I can focus on the Son.

Easter

Longsuffering is the howling season of a wintery tomb;
Lamentations and wailing, the sounds of a stark raving loon.

Collapsing anguish and weariness as the dark coffin steals
the light;
Fire consumes with blistering heat in the furnace of the night.

The malaise is unyielding, it will rob the flesh off your bones;
Death brings the haymaker and covers you in stones.

But wait! A whist rises to the surface, the voice of One
from above;
He reaches below the grassy dirt and offers His arms of LOVE.

The winter is over and Easter has shown;
He breaks the chains and LIFE He has grown!

Deep within that heart once despairing;
Now full of rapture and sparkle, so daring.

Spring is in bloom and this heart has risen;
Like flowers once covered but now bundled and given.

No tears, only mirthful bliss adorn this cheerful face;
Hope has filled this soul and now the merriest of days.

Spice

Fire flies light up the night;
Sugar and spice are out of sight.

The trees beam with luminaries;
My heart wants to sing like a canary.

The fireworks are sensational as they shoot across the sky;
Makes me think of heaven but I don't want to die.

I am riding so high;
Eyes are wide.

Could stay up all night;
This thrill is like a light.

Burning bright in the trees and through the dark;
All I see are the sparks.

Makes me forget the mental suffering;
Cheers and laughter are all that ring.

True in my ears are the joyous laughs and cries;
It is not a full moon thank God or else I might hide.

But I just ride the vibe;
It is like music or some type of jive.

Romance fills the air and love spills over the lawn;
I love this ability to feel things; I will stay out until dawn.

Bee's Knees

Bees fly and swarm up high;
The bee's knees cannot tell a lie.

The bee's knees means "the height of excellence;"
Like royalty or even a prince.

A life with God is much the same;
No matter the struggle, no matter the pain.

We are royal from His palace above;
Even when we mourn just like the doves.

Whatever we are feeling, it is only fleeting;
Nothing changes the fact that one day we will be meeting.

Face to face we shall gaze;
Far away from the maize.

Keep your eye on the prize;
When you want to die.

Remember that life looks worst,
When you forget who is first.

He rescued you and dusted you off;
He will carry you through when you feel engulfed.

Rise and take your position at His court;
Hold your head high and ride from the fort!

PART TWO

Jesus

Like a red rose in its brilliant beauty;
The drops of blood came forth for His duty.

The crimson stains that made us well;
They cost a lot and kept us from hell.

He was scarred beyond measure and beaten too;
He did it for us and He did it for you.

The crown of thorns smashed into His head;
They left Him for dead.

But He was being guided by the Father's hand;
He would soon help us enter the Promised Land.

The cross was too heavy attached to His back;
His knees would buckle and O they would smack...

The ground they would hit and tear them apart;
How could He continue, why did He have to start.

This journey was planned before time began;
The Father sustained Him and took His hand.

The violence of it all, the flesh falling on the ground;
He did not say a word; He did not make a sound.

He saw us in a broken state, wicked and poor... such
  degenerates.
He looked beyond all of the mess and the sea of sin and hate.

He stretched out His arms on that tree.
His legs were pinned with stakes; it was the fee.

The fee for us to have life now and forevermore;
That rose lost its ravishing petals, they hit the floor.

That red rose was crushed but spilled out with such a
fragrance.
He was bruised but yet the aroma remains so now we
must dance.

Prayer of Salvation and Baptism of the Holy Spirit

"Father, I know that I have sinned and broken Your laws. I know that this has separated me from You. I am truly sorry and I want to turn from my past sinful life and live for you. Please forgive me and help me to live a godly life. I believe that Jesus Christ died for my sins, was raised from the dead, is alive, and hears my cry right now. I invite Jesus to become the Lord of my life, to rule and to reign in my heart every day of my life. I ask for Your Holy Spirit to baptize me and live in me, helping me to obey You and do Your will. As evidence of this change I ask for the gifts of the Holy Spirit and most importantly the fruit of the Holy Spirit to manifest itself in my life. Help me to live out my calling here on earth. Please right my name down in the Lamb's book of life. Thank you for my salvation. In Jesus' name I pray, Amen."

What works for me...

1. I have a Relationship with Jesus
2. I always take my medicine
3. I always see my doctor
4. I watch lots of comedies
5. I try to never judge myself
6. I tell myself that I rock every day
7. I cry out to God a lot
8. I reach out to somebody the second I start feeling bad; I never hold it in
9. I call 911 or go to the hospital if I am struggling with suicidal thoughts
10. I got involved in church and particularly two small groups that have carried me many times
11. I never self medicate
12. I try to never compare myself to others
13. I let others lay down their lives for me when it was all I could do to barely function
14. I went to a few support groups
15. I have ongoing counseling
16. I am very transparent about my issues with kind, safe individuals that I trust
17. Often I just rest and breathe deeply to relax and be still
18. I speak the scriptures out loud when my mind is out of control
19. Exercise
20. Take one day at a time
21. I prayed and prayed for a good doctor and never gave up the search
22. I do things for others to get my mind off of myself
23. I journal at times

24. I go camping by the lake and skiing to see God's creation
25. I try and embrace my humanity every day
26. I hug myself and try to cheer myself on
27. I read the promises of God every day
28. I write because it is my passion and makes me feel alive
29. I am asking God to help me be okay in my own skin each day
30. I have deep personal friendships with hysterical people that love me as I am

Notes

1. Zondervan NIV Study Bible. Fully rev. ed. Kenneth L. Barker. Gen. ed Grand Rapids, MI: Zondervan, 2002.
2. See 1 Corinthians 2:16.
3. See 2 Corinthians 10:5.
4. See John 19:2.
5. See Genesis 15:18-21.
6. See Matthew 10:42.
7. See Genesis 9:13.
8. See Revelation 13:8.
9. See John 15:19.
10. See Psalm 118:6.
11. See Romans 8:12-14.
12. See Jeremiah 29:11.
13. See Genesis 1:11-13.
14. See Isaiah 53.
15. See John 3:16.
16. See Psalm 141:8.
17. See Philippians 4:8
18. See Psalm 32:10.
19. See Psalm 51:17.
20. See Psalm 150:1.
21. See Ephesians 6:16.
22. See Psalm 147:3.
23. See 2 Corinthians 6:2.
24. See Lamentations 3:22, 23.
25. See Matthew 19:26.
26. See 2 Corinthians 10:4.
27. See 1 Corinthians 9:24.
28. See Isaiah 65:25.
29. See Romans 8:37.

30. See Luke 11:9.
31. See Song of Solomon 2:14.
32. See Psalm 45:11.
33. See John 8:36.
34. See Hosea.
35. See John 11:1-53.
36. C.S Lewis, The Screwtape Letters (New York: Macmillan, 1961),59.
37. Poem Zest inspired by Joel Osteen
38. Movie title Snatch (same name).
39. Rock, Paper, Scissors taken from an old hand game.
40. Bee's Knees taken from the 1920's terminology meaning created with brilliance or the height of excellence.
41. The famous yellow smiley face taken from the 1963 kids show The Funny Company.
42. Harbor in the storm taken from U2's song One.
43. Dorothy's Pocket taken from Dorothy Holloway.
44. Reference to my Dell laptop taken from Dell.

Made in the
USA
Columbia, SC